Messages of Faith from the Bible

...with God all things are possible

The C.R. Gibson Company, Norwalk, Connecticut

The Essence of Faith

Jesus saith unto him, Thomas, because thou hast seen me, thou hast believed: blessed are they that have not seen, and yet have believed.

John 20:29

Now faith is the substance of things hoped for, the evidence of things not seen.
Through faith we understand that the worlds were framed by the word of God, so that things which are seen were not made of things which do appear.

Hebrews 11:1,3

Blessed be the God and Father of our Lord Jesus Christ, which according to his abundant mercy hath begotten us again unto a lively hope by the resurrection of Jesus Christ from the dead. Whom having not seen, ye love; in whom, though now ye see him not, yet believing, ye rejoice with joy unspeakable and full of glory.

I Peter 1:3,8

The things which are impossible with men are possible with God.

Luke 18:27

All things are possible to him that believeth.

Mark 9:23

If ye have faith as a grain of mustard seed, ye
shall say unto this mountain, Remove hence
to yonder place; and it shall remove; and
nothing shall be impossible unto you.

Matthew 17:20

I delight to do thy will, O my God: yea, thy law
is within my heart.

Psalm 40:8

I can do all things through Christ which
strengtheneth me.

Philippians 4:13

For with thee is the fountain of life: in thy
light shall we see light.

Psalm 36:9

Arise, go thy way: thy faith hath made thee whole.

Luke 17:19

The Power
of Faith

Ask, and it shall be given you; seek, and ye shall find; knock, and it shall be opened unto you.

Matthew 7:7

Therefore I say unto you, What things soever ye desire, when ye pray, believe that ye receive them, and ye shall have them.

Mark 11:24

The Lord is nigh unto all them that call upon him, to all that call upon him in truth.

Psalm 145:18

Then shall ye call upon me, and ye shall go and pray unto me, and I will hearken unto you.
And ye shall seek me, and find me, when ye shall search for me with all your heart.

Jeremiah 29:12-13

And whatsoever ye shall ask in my name, that will I do, that the Father may be glorified in the Son.
If ye shall ask any thing in my name, I will do it.

John 14:13-14

O give thanks unto the Lord; for he is good: because his mercy endureth for ever.

Psalm 118:1

The Lord is my light and my salvation; whom shall
I fear?

Psalm 27:1

There is no fear in love; but perfect love casteth
out fear.

1 John 4:18

And we know that all things work together for
good to them that love God, to them who are
the called according to his purpose.

Romans 8:28

Know ye that the Lord he is God: it is he that
hath made us, and not we ourselves; we are
his people, and the sheep of his pasture.
For the Lord is good; his mercy is everlasting;
and his truth endureth to all generations.

Psalm 100:3,5

The just shall live by his faith.

Habakkuk 2:4

The Comfort
of Faith

The Lord is my shepherd; I shall not want.

Psalm 23:1

I am the resurrection, and
the life: he that believeth in me, though he
were dead, yet shall he live.

John 11:25

Trust ye in the Lord for ever: for in the Lord
Jehovah is everlasting strength.

Isaiah 26:4

Consider the lilies of the field, how they grow;
they toil not, neither do they spin:
And yet I say unto you, That even Solomon in all
his glory was not arrayed like one of these.

Matthew 6:28-29

Behold the fowls of the air: for they sow not,
neither do they reap, nor gather into barns;
yet your heavenly Father feedeth them.

Matthew 6:26

If I take the wings of the morning, and dwell in
the uttermost parts of the sea;
Even there shall thy hand lead me, and thy right
hand shall hold me.

Psalm 139:9-10

I am like a green olive tree in the house of
God: I trust in the mercy of God for ever
and ever.

Psalm 52:8

Peace I leave with you, my peace I give unto you:
not as the world giveth, give I unto you.
Let not your heart be troubled, neither let
it be afraid.

John 14:27

Behold, I stand at the door, and knock: if any
man hear my voice, and open the door, I will
come in to him, and will sup with him, and he
with me.

Revelation 3:20

For where two or three are gathered together in
my name, there am I in the midst of them.

Matthew 18:20

Be strong and of a good courage; be not afraid,
neither be thou dismayed: for the Lord thy
God is with thee whithersoever thou goest.

Joshua 1:9

The Joy of Faith

Ye are blessed of the Lord which made heaven and earth.

Psalm 115:15

The earth is full of the goodness of the Lord.

Psalm 33:5

Thou wilt shew me the path of life: in thy presence is fulness of joy; at thy right hand there are pleasures for evermore.

Psalm 16:11

Delight thyself also in the Lord; and he shall give thee the desires of thine heart.

Psalm 37:4

Hitherto have ye asked nothing in my name: ask, and ye shall receive, that your joy may be full.

John 16:24

I love the Lord, because he hath heard my voice and my supplications.
Because he hath inclined his ear unto me, therefore will I call upon him as long as I live.

Psalm 116:1-2

Every good gift and every perfect gift is from above, and cometh down from the Father.

James 1:17

The Lord is good unto them that wait for him, to
the soul that seeketh him.

Lamentations 3:25

I love them that love me; and those that seek me
early shall find me.

Proverbs 8:17

This is the day which the Lord hath made; we will
rejoice and be glad in it.

Psalm 118:24

Rejoice with them that do rejoice.

Romans 12:15

The fruit of the Spirit is love, joy, peace,
longsuffering, gentleness, goodness, faith.

Galatians 5:22

For the kingdom of God is not meat and drink; but
righteousness, and peace, and joy in the
Holy Ghost.

Romans 14:17

Surely goodness and mercy shall follow me all the
days of my life: and I will dwell in the house of
the Lord for ever.

Psalm 23:6

The Covenant
of Faith

And God said, This is the token of the covenant which I make between me and you and every living creature that is with you, for perpetual generations:
I do set my bow in the cloud, and it shall be for a token of a covenant between me and the earth.

Genesis 9:12-13

Thy mercy, O Lord, is in the heavens; and thy faithfulness reacheth unto the clouds.
How excellent is thy lovingkindness, O God! therefore the children of men put their trust under the shadow of thy wings.

Psalm 36:5,7

God is our refuge and strength, a very present help in trouble.

Psalm 46:1

The eternal God is thy refuge, and underneath are the everlasting arms.

Deuteronomy 33:27

The Lord is my rock, and my fortress, and
my deliverer;
The God of my rock; in him will I trust: he is my
shield, and the horn of my salvation, my
high tower, and my refuge, my saviour.

2 Samuel 22:2-3

The Lord will give strength unto his people;
the Lord will bless his people with peace.

Psalm 29:11

And ye now therefore have sorrow: but I will see
you again, and your heart shall rejoice, and your
joy no man taketh from you.

John 16:22

I will not leave you comfortless: I will come
to you.

John 14:18

The Lord is my strength and my shield; my heart
trusted in him, and I am helped.

Psalm 28:7

The Triumph of Faith

For God so loved the world, that he gave his only begotten Son, that whosoever believeth in him should not perish, but have everlasting life.

John 3:16

I am the good shepherd.

John 10:11

My sheep hear my voice, and I know them, and they follow me:
And I give unto them eternal life; and they shall never perish, neither shall any man pluck them out of my hand.

John 10:27-28

For whoso findeth me findeth life, and shall obtain favour of the Lord.

Proverbs 8:35

Let not your heart be troubled: ye believe in God, believe also in me.
In my Father's house are many mansions: if it were not so, I would have told you. I go to prepare a place for you.

John 14:1-2

Every one that hath forsaken houses, or brethren, or sisters, or father, or mother, or wife, or children, or lands, for my name's sake, shall receive an hundredfold, and shall inherit everlasting life.

Matthew 19:29

I am the light of the world: he that followeth me shall not walk in darkness, but shall have the light of life.

John 8:12

For thou wilt light my candle: the Lord my God will enlighten my darkness.

Psalm 18:28

He that soweth to the Spirit shall of the Spirit reap life everlasting.

Galatians 6:8

Lo, I am with you alway, even unto the end of the world.

Matthew 28:20

Selected by Jayne Bowman
Designed by Bob Pantelone

Set in Paladium/Helios

Photo Credits

Klauss Brahmst—cover, pp.4,5; Pat Powers—p.6; Wyoming—p.9; Florida—p.10; Robert Grana—p.13; ALPHA—p.14; James Patrick—p.17; Three Lions—p.18; Kathe Gendel—p.21; James Power—p.22; Jeff Munk—p.25; Elizabeth Welsh—p.26; Robert Martin—p.29; Four By Five— endpapers.